Hard Choices

Hard Choices

On the road to Calvary

Tony Kidd

Scripture Union

Scripture Union, 207-209 Queensway, Bletchley, MK2 2EB, England.
email: info@scriptureunion.org.uk
Internet: http://www.scripture.org.uk/

© Tony Kidd

First published 1999

ISBN 1 85999 385 0

The Scripture quotations contained herein are from the New Revised
Standard Version Bible, copyright © 1989 by the Division of Christian
Education of the National Council of the Churches of Christ in the
USA, and are used by permission. All rights reserved.

British Library Cataloguing-in-Publication Data
A catalogue record for this book is available from the British Library.

Cover design by Julian Smith.
Illustrations by Neil Reed/Allied Artists/London.
Printed and bound in Great Britain by Creative Print and Design,
(Wales) Ebbw Vale.

Contents

Introduction

Every day of our lives we make choices, some of them conscious, others not. We do so based on what we have been taught and what we have learned from experience over the years.

When Jesus chose to face crucifixion, he made a choice that will echo into eternity. He made his decision based on the principles that had guided his whole life.

How great is our awareness of the implications of choices we make? Do we examine them through the eyes of Jesus? Do we allow the Bible to guide us as we choose? Are we ready to face the conflict, within ourselves and with others, which may arise because of the choices we make?

This course has been written primarily for use by groups, although it may also be helpful to individuals. A group of six to ten people is ideal. Group members may like to appoint a leader, or take it in turns over the six weeks to be responsible for facilitating the group and keeping time. Allow between one-and-a-half and two hours for each session. Suggested timings for the specific sections are:

Way in.........10–15 minutes   Response .....15–20 minutes
Bible ....20–30 minutes   Prayer...........10–20 minutes
Life................5–10 minutes

Included are suggestions for songs which reflect the theme for each session, and these can be found in Mission Praise (MP), Songs of Fellowship (SOF) and Let's Praise (LP). There are also suggestions for music to be played when leading into times of prayer or during the meditations. Catalogue information for the recordings selected are as follows:

Choir of New College Oxford, *Agnus Dei: Music of inner harmony*, Warner Music No. 0630-14634-2.
Silence, SONYTV35CD, 31-489012-10
Meditations at Sunset, Nimbus NI 7010.
Adiemus, *Songs of Sanctuary*, CDVE 925 7243 8 40428 2 0.
Enya, *Shepherd Moons*, 9031-75572-2
Iona, *The Book of Kells*, WHAC 1287.

The Bible passages (from the New Revised Standard Version of the Bible) are printed in full. The group may prefer to read these in silence. Alternatively:

• One person reads the passage aloud while the others listen.

• Two or three people read alternate verses.

• One person takes the role of narrator while others read any dialogue.

The meditations can be approached in three ways:

• You may like to read them on your own silently or, if no one else is near, out loud.

• If you are in a group, one person might read the meditation to the others. The passage should be read slowly, with pauses at appropriate points to allow time for people to take in the atmosphere and bring their imaginations into play.

• If the person reading to the group is feeling fairly confident, they might use the meditation as a basis for painting their own picture of the scene, pausing after each line to inject imagery or description.

An illustration appears near some meditations, to provide a focus; but you may like to bring an appropriate object such as a spray of leaves or flowers, a cross or a candle. Other pictures, either photographs or prints of paintings, can be used. Be creative in thinking up ways to bring interest and variety to each session.

Note

- At times of sharing, no one should feel obliged to say more than they want to, and individual privacy must always be respected. As a group, be sensitive to the possibility that some members may find parts of the sessions difficult. Providing support in such circum- stances may be helpful.

- There are opportunities in the sessions for times of silence, for example during prayer or after reading a Bible passage or meditation. Some may find silence uncomfortable, so offer reassurance beforehand. Let peo- ple know how long the silence will last, and that they can use it for quiet prayer, to unburden themselves from the pressures of the day, or simply to be still before God.

Prayer times will give people the opportunity to share with the rest of the group anything that has been particularly significant for them during the session, and to pray about it together. Further reflection will be aided by using the readings for the week and the pattern of prayer outlined on pages 19–20. The pattern of prayer is designed for use each day during the course, and may be adapted to suit personal taste and practice. The daily readings form a natural part of the pattern of prayer. You may wish to use these, along with the words of praise and the meditations, as a group, or individually throughout the week.

The key questions act as a starting point for reflection in the days immediately after the meeting.

The following are the readings for the three days before the first meeting:

Preparation	Day 1	Psalm 37:1–40, There is a future for the peaceable
	Day 2	Psalm 50:1–23, The wicked hate God's discipline
	Day 3	Jeremiah 8:4–12, There is no peace
Meeting	**Day 4**	**John 15:18 – 16:14, The world will reject the disciples**

Session 1

Choices in a world of conflict

Aim

To think about how we cope with a world in which more people have been killed in the last hundred years than were alive in Jesus' day.

Way in

Talk with a neighbour about the way you deal with the images of conflict and suffering you see on television or in newspapers. Then spend time praying together about the issues this raises, or about anything else you or your partner wish to bring before God.

Songs to sing

'Do not be afraid', MP 115.
'For I'm building a people of power', MP 151, SOF 111, LP 37.
'Hail, thou once despisèd Jesus', MP 203, SOF 149.
'How I love You', MP 246, SOF 190, LP 69.
'Lead us, heavenly Father, lead us', MP 400, SOF 321.
'Led like a lamb to the slaughter', MP 402, SOF 322, LP 105.
'Living under the shadow of His wing', MP 423, SOF 346.
'The price is paid', MP 663, LP 206.
'Who is on the Lord's side?', MP 769, SOF 607.

Music to listen to

Gorecki: 'Totus Tous', from *Agnus Dei*.
Mahler: Symphony No. 5 (Adagietto), from *Silence* (part only).
Iona: 'Luke – The Calf', from *The Book of Kells*.

Bible

John 15:18 – 16:14, Jesus tells his disciples that the world will reject them

[18] 'If the world hates you, be aware that it hated me before it hated you. [19] If you belonged to the world, the world would love you as its own. Because you do not belong to the world, but I have chosen you out of the world – therefore the world hates you. [20] Remember the word that I said to you, "Servants are not greater than their master." If they persecuted me, they will persecute you; if they kept my word, they will keep yours also. [21] But they will do all these things to you on account of my name, because they do not know him who sent me. [22] If I had not come and spoken to them, they would not have sin; but now they have no excuse for their sin. [23] Whoever hates me hates my Father also. [24] If I had not done among them the works that no one else did, they would not have sin. But now they have seen and hated both me and my Father. [25] It was to fulfil the word that is written in their law, "They hated me without a cause."

[26] 'When the Advocate comes, whom I will send to you from the Father, the Spirit of truth who comes from the Father, he will testify on my behalf. [27] You also are to testify because you have been with me from the beginning.

16 'I have said these things to you to keep you from stumbling. [2] They will put you out of the synagogues. Indeed, an hour is coming when those who kill you will think that by doing so they are offering worship to God. [3] And they will do this because they have not known the Father or me. [4] But I have said these things to you so that when their hour comes you may remember that I told you about them.

'I did not say these things to you from the beginning, because I was with you. [5] But now I am going to him who sent me; yet none of you asks me, "Where are you going?" [6] But because I have said these things to you, sorrow has filled your hearts. [7] Nevertheless I tell you the truth: it is to your advantage that I go away, for if I do not go away, the Advocate will not come to you; but if I go, I will send him to you. [8] And when he comes, he will prove the world wrong about sin and righteousness and judgment: ⁹ about sin, because they do not believe in me; ¹⁰ about righteousness, because I am going to the Father and you will see me no longer; ¹¹ about judgment, because the ruler of this world has been condemned.

¹² 'I still have many things to say to you, but you cannot bear them now. ¹³ When the Spirit of truth comes, he will guide you into all truth; for he will not speak on his own, but will speak whatever he hears, and he will declare to you the things that are to come. ¹⁴ He will glorify me, because he will take what is mine and declare it to you.'

The choice of faith

When Jesus spoke of the world hating him, he was particularly conscious that he was opposed every step of the way by those in authority. In Western Europe generally, and Great Britain especially, Jesus would surely have much the same reception today. Thus, as he prayed for his disciples, he did so acknowledging that theirs had been a difficult path and that it would not get any easier. They had chosen change and obedience, both hard to accept, especially when others are not necessarily sympathetic to those decisions or their outcome. Jesus' prayer is designed to prepare the disciples for the rocky path of continuing to be different just as he is different. The establishment of his day could not cope with his challenge to the accepted social and religious order. In the same way, Jesus' teaching is at odds with much of the world through which it travels today.

As Christians, we discover that the way chosen by the disciples is just as hard to take now as it was two thousand years ago. It is the way of taking only what we need rather than all that we desire. Resisting what St John calls 'the lust of the eyes' (1 John 2:16) is not easy, nor is living in a world where being different from our neighbours can cause significant problems.

Meditation

THE CHOICE OF LOVE

I choose only what I need and sacrifice what I want.
My need above all else is to be obedient,
but sometimes and all too easily the real need is obscured
by the counterfeit which is desire.
I choose love.

I choose the person not the prejudice.
Obedience makes me blind to colour, tribe or legalistic religion.
I see only what my Father loves
and that will be my guide.
I choose love.

I choose my Father's family, not merely the kinship of blood.
Obedience lies in recognising the Spirit in all things
and in being free to experience the ties
that bind in heavenly eternity.
I choose love.

I give and do not look for reward.
I do not choose the easy way but the right one.
I dare to face change and the unfamiliar
if that is where the pathway leads.
I choose love.

I choose to be obedient.
I may physically die in that choice,
but I will live in the eternity of the faith by which I choose.
I will take up my cross and follow where my Father leads.
I choose love.

Discussion

How hard is it to be loving when there is conflict facing you at home, at work or in the world? Share with the rest of the group a situation from your own life in which you have encountered such a dilemma.

Life

However hard we may try, it is impossible for most of us to ignore the fact that we live in a world where conflict is rarely far beneath the surface. The Balkans, the Middle East, Kashmir and Northern Ireland are just some of the examples in this century that spring to mind. Spend a few minutes thinking about your reactions to conflict, whether at home or abroad. Then do the following exercise.

Coping with conflict

Myself

Do I ever feel overwhelmed when I hear of refugees, ethnic cleansing and other features of modern warfare? If so, how do I deal with it?

What part does prayer play in my response to the violence in our world?

Others

What practical steps can I take, with others, which might make a difference?

Are others already involved? Can I help?

Response

Share with the group one thing you have discovered during the 'Life' section. Pray together for the places, countries or people featured in this section, and your responses to their situations.

Key question

Can I love my neighbour better than I do?

Praise

Leader: The Lord rescues us from our enemies.

All: We serve him without fear.

Leader: In holiness and righteousness before him...

All: We serve him without fear.

Leader: Because of his tender mercy...

All: He guides us into the path of peace.

(Based on Luke 1:74–75,79)

Meditation

How should I make my choice
between this army and that one?
Are the bullets softer when fired by a man I know?
Does the bomb kill fewer people
when it is dropped by a plane I helped to buy?
Is land more wholesome when we kill to live on it?
Is a nation more civilised
when it destroys others to support itself?
Do we build our houses on sand
when we forget to love our neighbours
and choose to kill them for the cause?

Readings for the week

1. Choices in a world of conflict		
Reflection	Day 5	Matthew 24:1–14, All nations will hate you
	Day 6	Matthew 5:1–12, Rejoice at persecution
	Day 7	Romans 5:1–11, Peace and reconciliation
2. Choices in a needy world		
Preparation	Day 1	Deuteronomy 15:7–11, Be open-handed
	Day 2	Psalm 107:1–43, God's response to the needy
	Day 3	Proverbs 30:7–9,12–14, Devouring those in need
Meeting	**Day 4**	**John 6:1–13, The loaves and the fish**

Pattern of prayer

You may like to use this pattern as a basis for your daily prayers during the course.

Praise and thanksgiving
Spend a few moments thinking of the things you want to thank God for, then offer them up to him in praise.

I will sing to the Lord,
    for he is highly exalted.
I will sing to the Lord,
    he has become my salvation.
I will sing to the Lord,
    and I will praise him.

(Based on Exodus 15:1–2)

Confession
Spend a few moments thinking of things you need to confess, asking for forgiveness.

Seek the Lord while he may be found;
    Our God will freely pardon.
Call on the Lord while he is near;
    Our God will freely pardon.
Let us confess our sins to the Lord;
    Our God will freely pardon.

(Based on Isaiah 55:6)

Bible

On each day when you are preparing for the next session, read the Bible passage and spend time reflecting on it, making notes of any feelings you experience.

or

On each day when you are reflecting on the last session, reread the key Bible passage for the session and make notes of any new thoughts or feelings you have.

then

Use the reading for the day, or one of the meditations for the week to come, and be still before God.

Intercession

Bring to God:

* any people or situations that you feel need his love
* the other members of the group
* your own needs

The Lord's Prayer

Our Father in heaven,
hallowed be your name,
your kingdom come,
your will be done on earth,
as it is in heaven.
Give us today our daily bread.
Forgive us our sins
as we forgive those who sin against us.
Lead us not into temptation
but deliver us from evil.
For the kingdom, the power and the glory are yours
now and forever. Amen.

In closing

Lord, let me go out in the peace of Jesus Christ. In his name I ask it. Amen.

Session 2

Choices in a needy world

Aim

To consider how we choose between our own needs and those of others.

Way in

Spend a few minutes talking with another member of the group about a situation where you have faced difficulty in reconciling your needs or desires with those of others. Pray together about the issues this raises, or about anything else you or your partner wish to bring before God.

Songs to sing
'Amazing grace', MP 31, SOF 19, LP 6.
'An army of ordinary people', MP 32, SOF 20.
'Christ is the answer', MP 72.
'Darkness like a shroud', MP 110, SOF 78, LP 27.
'Give me a heart', MP 165.
'Healing God, Almighty Father', MP 226.
'Lord, have mercy on us', MP 430, SOF 354, LP 118.
'Restore, O Lord', MP 579, SOF 483, LP 172.
'We have a gospel to proclaim', MP 728, LP 220.
'What a friend we have in Jesus', MP 746, SOF 593.
'You are the vine', MP 792, SOF 629.

Music to listen to
Palestrina: 'Kyrie' (*Missa Papae Marcelli*), from *Agnus Dei*.

Elgar: Serenade in E minor op. 20 (Larghetto), from *Meditations at Sunset*.

Enya: 'Evacuee', from *Shepherd Moons*.

Bible

John 6:1–13, The loaves and the fish

6 After this Jesus went to the other side of the Sea of Galilee, also called the Sea of Tiberias. ² A large crowd kept following him, because they saw the signs that he was doing for the sick. ³ Jesus went up the mountain and sat down there with his disciples. ⁴ Now the Passover, the festival of the Jews, was near. ⁵ When he looked up and saw a large crowd coming toward him, Jesus said to Philip, 'Where are we to buy bread for these people to eat?' ⁶ He said this to test him, for he himself knew what he was going to do. ⁷ Philip answered him, 'Six months' wages would not buy enough bread for each of them to get a little.' ⁸ One of his disciples, Andrew, Simon Peter's brother, said to him, ⁹ 'There is a boy here who has five barley loaves and two fish. But what are they among so many people?' ¹⁰ Jesus said, 'Make the people sit down.' Now there was a great deal of grass in the place; so they sat down, about five thousand in all. ¹¹ Then Jesus took the loaves, and when he had given thanks, he distributed them to those who were seated; so also the fish, as much as they wanted. ¹² When they were satisfied, he told his disciples, 'Gather up the fragments left over, so that nothing may be lost.' ¹³ So they gathered them up, and from the fragments of the five barley loaves, left by those who had eaten, they filled twelve baskets.

The boy's choice

What would have happened if the boy in the story of the loaves and fishes had chosen to eat his meal instead of giving it to Jesus? We are not told very much about the lad, but we know he came to listen to Jesus better prepared for a day out than many others in the crowd. We also know he made a vital choice when he trusted Jesus enough to hand over his provisions.

We can contrast the boy's response in this incident with that of the rich young man of Matthew 19:16–22: he went away down-cast. To what extent are we prepared to give up what we have and to trust Jesus? Can we bring ourselves to believe him when he says in Matthew 19:29 that we will receive much more in exchange for what we give?

The following meditation, on another example of generosity from the Gospels, may help us sift out some of the issues raised here.

Meditation
(Matthew 21:14; Mark 12:41–44)

WHAT A BLIND MAN HEARS
Because I am blind
I hear all sorts of things that help me to see.
I've never actually seen the woman
who put two tiny coins in the Treasury,
but I know what she is like.
The money went in very quietly –
in fact, I only just heard it.
She never makes any fuss –
just one quick movement and the coins are gone.
Not like the man over there,
making all that noise, drawing attention to himself,
jangling his purse so as to be sure we all hear.
He will have long robes and a heavy embroidered cloak;
she will be in faded black.
He will give his tithe to the exact penny
and have plenty to spare;
she has nothing left now.
He will always want more;
she has all she needs and is content.
He takes more than he needs or deserves;
she relies on washing and cleaning for others
to get what she needs to live.
She will come back next week, she always does.
I look forward to her coming –

it means that God has not let her down.
She makes a difference,
because what she gives comes quietly,
with grace and spirit, from her heart.
God can multiply that.
God takes her small coins, fits them into their proper space,
and they make his plan complete.
For God, nothing is too small;
no one is unimportant –
not a small coin, not a widow,
nor a blind man who sees and prays in his heart.

Discussion

Can you think of any contemporary examples of the boy, the rich
young man or the woman? Do you think Jesus would see them
differently from the way the world does? How would he view
them?

Life

Spend a few minutes taking stock of your lifestyle and how you
feel about it. Then explore a few of the choices you have made in
the past, or which may be open to you now or in the near future.
Use the following model to consider the question, 'How do I live,
and what does it cost me and others?'

Lifestyle choices

Myself
What am I able to do?

What have I done to deserve it?

_____

Others
How does what I do benefit others?

_____

Do I think about my choices and the way they affect others? If so, how?

_____

Response
Without feeling that you have to disclose any of the detail of your thoughts, discuss together any discoveries you have made during the session which have altered your view of your choices.

Where choices have had a negative effect on people's lives, this may be a good opportunity to seek forgiveness or to offer forgiveness in prayer to others.

Key questions
During the week ahead consider the following questions:

_____

- Can you identify any choices you could make, at a personal level, which might make a positive difference to the lives of others? For example, giving up a week's holiday away and using the cash saved to help a charity to which you are committed.

- Do you have a 'I'll be happy when...' attitude to life? Can you think of any choices you could make in the future, which might alter this?

Praise

Leader: Come, all you who are thirsty.
All: Let us go to the waters of life.
Leader: Come and buy without cost.
All: Let us go to the waters of life.
Leader: Your soul will delight in the richest fare.
All: Let us listen that our souls may live.

(Based on Isaiah 55:1–3)

Meditation

I want a new car –
but, for the price, I could buy a hundred bicycles
for those who have to walk.

I want a new car –
but, for the price, I could buy ten dwellings
for those who have no home.

We want a new player for the team –
but, for the price, we could buy a thousand motor cars.

We need a new set of values –
how much will that cost?

Readings for the week

2. Choices in a needy world		
Reflection	Day 5	Matthew 6:1–6, Give to the needy
	Day 6	2 Corinthians 9:6–15, Be generous
	Day 7	1 Timothy 6:11–19, Be ready to share

3. Choices in a materialistic world		
Preparation	Day 1	1 Samuel 8:1–22, Choosing the world
	Day 2	Psalm 17:1–15, The prayer of a righteous man
	Day 3	Hosea 14:1–9, Return to the right way
Meeting	**Day 4**	**Matthew 20:1–16, The workers in the vineyard**

Session 3

Choices in a materialistic world

Aim
To consider the dilemmas we face at work and in our daily lives.

Way in
Discuss with your neighbour a situation at work or domestically where you have encountered difficulties, for example with unhelpful employers, colleagues or commercial practice. Spend time praying together about the issues this raises, or about anything else you or your partner wish to bring before God.

Songs to sing
'Come, let us join our cheerful songs', MP 93, SOF 70.
'Fear not, rejoice and be glad', MP 144, SOF 106.
'How precious, O Lord', MP 252, SOF 193.
'I'd rather have Jesus', MP 319.
'Immortal, invisible', MP 327, SOF 234, LP 88.
'Joy to the world!', MP 393, SOF 314, LP 102.
'Lord, you are more precious than silver', MP 447, SOF 368.
'Rejoice, rejoice! Christ is in you', MP 572, SOF 480, LP 169.
'Take my life, and let it be', MP 624, SOF 519, LP 193.
'Turn your eyes upon Jesus', MP 712.

Music to listen to
Elgar: 'Lux Aeterna' (Nimrod), from *Agnus Dei*.
Gluck: 'Dance of the Blessed Spirits' (*Orfeo ed Euridice*), from *Silence*.

Iona: Opening Theme ('I stand on ground'), from *The Book of Kells*.

Bible

Matthew 20:1–16, The workers in the vineyard

20 'For the kingdom of heaven is like a landowner who went out early in the morning to hire labourers for his vineyard. ² After agreeing with the labourers for the usual daily wage, he sent them into his vineyard. ³ When he went out about nine o'clock, he saw others standing idle in the marketplace; ⁴ and he said to them, 'You also go into the vineyard, and I will pay you whatever is right.' So they went. ⁵ When he went out again about noon and about three o'clock, he did the same. ⁶ And about five o'clock he went out and found others standing around; and he said to them, 'Why are you standing here idle all day?' ⁷ They said to him, 'Because no one has hired us.' He said to them, 'You also go into the vineyard.' ⁸ When evening came, the owner of the vineyard said to his manager, 'Call the labourers and give them their pay, beginning with the last and then going to the first.' ⁹ When those hired about five o'clock came, each of them received the usual daily wage. ¹⁰ Now when the first came, they thought they would receive more; but each of them also received the usual daily wage. ¹¹ And they grumbled against the landowner, ¹² saying, 'these last worked only one hour, and you have made them equal to us who have borne the burden of the day and the scorching heat.' ¹³ But he replied to one of them, 'Friend, I am doing you no wrong; did you not agree with me for the usual daily wage? ¹⁴ Take what belongs to you and go; I choose to give to this last the same as I give to you. ¹⁵ Am I not allowed to do what I choose with what belongs to me? Or are you envious because I am generous?' ¹⁶ So the last will be first, and the first will be last.'

The landowner's choice

It is so easy to follow the ways of the world. For example, equal pay for equal work sounds sensible when we focus on the pay, but what about when we turn to the work? Suppose we have worked longer than the next person? Is equal pay then a fair wage? Our natural sympathy may well be with the workers who complained rather than the landowner. But the rewards of God's kingdom are made equally available to the lifelong follower of Jesus and the latecomer who turns to him at the end of life. It is a matter of grace, not earnings.

The choices Christians make can look strange to the worldly. We may, for example, choose to work harder, longer or for less reward. We may choose to run a business in which service rather than profit is maximised or we take out less than we want but as much as we need. Our employment may be with a less fashionable organisation but one which tries harder to respect its customers and the environment. If we look afresh at our situation, the number of options open to us may be more numerous than we presently choose to think.

Discussion
Spend a few minutes as a group discussing the position of the workers who had laboured throughout the day. Were they justified in complaining? Have you ever experienced anything similar?

Meditation
(Matthew 4:18–20)

PETER'S CHOICE TO BECOME A FISHER OF MEN
My life's been easy up 'til now.
No big questions or decisions, no choices to make.
I inherited the boat and my home,
the sea was on my doorstep,
I'd been taught the trade – what was there to decide?
After all, the fish bring in the money.
But, out of the blue, along comes this man Jesus.
I'd heard of him of course – who hadn't?
He'd caused quite a stir –
what with healings and getting
on the wrong side of the Pharisees.
But his ideas opened up new possibilities.
Not that I'd got any time to think about them much,

> but at least they were new, different, alive.
> Then, suddenly, here he is talking about fishing for men
> and giving me a decision to make, a choice.
> I'd always thought myself brave,
> but this would be a complete change.
> Do I have the courage to make it?
> Where will he go?
> Will I be any use to him?
> What does he mean about fishing for men?
> Why did he ask me?

Life

Take some time to reflect on the work you do. Do you work out of necessity (eg to pay the bills) or to fulfil your potential, exercise a right or for some other reason? Explore what you hope to give to others through your work and what they provide you with in return.

If you are not in paid work, consider these questions from the standpoint of how you spend your time. Then undertake the following analysis of your reflections.

Material choices

Myself
What does it cost me to work?

What benefits do I get from my work?

Others
How does my work benefit others?

What price do others pay for my work, and who are they?

Response

Discuss together any response to these questions which has surprised or encouraged you. Pray for individuals who face difficulties in their work, their frustrations as well as their hopes for the future.

Key question
Can you identify a choice open to you which would bring about a positive change in your own attitudes and actions, or those of others (for example, a shopping choice, a different approach to working practice)?

Praise

Leader: My soul glorifies the Lord.
All: My spirit rejoices in God my Saviour.
Leader: His mercy extends to those who fear him.
All: My spirit rejoices in God my Saviour.
Leader: He has filled the hungry with good things.
All: He has lifted up the humble.

(Based on Luke 1:46–53)

Meditation

Life will be better when
I have the next new thing that will give me
the feeling that I'm all right.

Life will be better when
the status I want is matched by
the things that ought to go with it.

Life will be better when
no one who matters to me
has more than I do.

But who am I beyond the things
that I allow to measure me?

Readings for the week

3. Choices in a materialistic world		
Reflection	Day 5	Acts 3:11–26, Peter explains the choice
	Day 6	1 John 2:15–17, Don't love the world
	Day 7	James 4:11–12, Who are you to judge?
4. Choosing to respect those who are different		
Preparation	Day 1	Ruth 2:1–23, Respect rewarded
	Day 2	Matthew 25:31–46, Welcoming strangers
	Day 3	Hebrews 13:1–6, Show hospitality
Meeting	**Day 4**	**Luke 10:25–37, The good Samaritan**

Session 4

Choosing to respect those who are different

Aim

To consider what choices we have in regard to our relationships with those of a different background from ourselves.

NB: In this session the phrase 'those of a different background' is intended to include social, cultural, racial or religious differences.

Way in

Share with a neighbour the extent to which you are conscious of significant background differences between yourself and others. How do you think you are perceived by others in this respect? Then spend time praying together about the issues this raises, or about anything else you or your partner wish to bring before God.

Songs to sing
'A new commandment', MP 1, SOF 22.
'Change my heart, O God', MP 69, SOF 58, LP 20.
'God forgave my sin', MP 181, SOF 129.
'Jesus, stand among us', MP 381, SOF 303.
'Jesus, you are changing me', MP 389, SOF 311.
'Let there be love shared among us', MP 411, SOF 329, LP 108.
'Make me a channel of Your peace', MP 456, SOF 381, LP 124.
'Spirit of the living God', MP 613, SOF 510.
'The King is among us', MP 650, SOF 532, LP 199.
'We your people' MP 741, LP 219.

Music to listen to
Mozart: 'Ave Verum Corpus', from *Agnus Dei.*
Finzi: Eclogue for piano & strings, from *Meditations at Sunset.*
Adiemus: 'Cantus Inaequalis', from *Songs of Sanctuary.*

Bible

Luke 10:25–37, The good Samaritan

25 Just then a lawyer stood up to test Jesus. 'Teacher,' he said, 'what must I do to inherit eternal life?' 26 He said to him, 'What is written in the law? What do you read there?' 27 He answered, 'You shall love the Lord your God with all your heart, and with all your soul, and with all your strength, and with all your mind; and your neighbour as yourself.' 28 And he said to him, 'You have given the right answer; do this, and you will live.'

29 But wanting to justify himself, he asked Jesus, 'And who is my neighbour?' 30 Jesus replied, 'A man was going down from Jerusalem to Jericho, and fell into the hands of robbers, who stripped him, beat him, and went away, leaving him half dead. 31 Now by chance a priest was going down that road; and when he saw him, he passed by on the other side. 32 So likewise a Levite, when he came to the place and saw him, passed by on the other side. 33 But a Samaritan while travelling came near him; and when he saw him, he was moved with pity. 34 He went to him and bandaged his wounds, having poured oil and wine on them. Then he put him on his own animal, brought him to an inn, and took care of him. 35 The next day he took out two denarii, gave them to the innkeeper, and said, 'Take care of him; and when I come back, I will repay you whatever more you spend.' 36 Which of these three, do you think, was a neighbour to the man who fell into the hands of the robbers?' 37 He said, 'The one who showed him mercy.' Jesus said to him, 'Go and do likewise.'

The Samaritan's choice

The priest and the Levite in this story made choices along lines that many still choose today. There are in every religion those in positions of leadership who will only attend to their own. The priest falls into that category; the Levite, a member of the priestly tribe and therefore closely associated with the priesthood, also fell far short of the test of neighbourliness Jesus requires. Each kept himself to himself rather than help a fellow human being. The man might be dead and, if he was, touching him would cause them to be ritually unclean (Numbers 19:11). The action of the Samaritan, a foreigner and from a people despised by the Jews, was all the more remarkable because the man was a Jew: at the time many Jews would add days to a journey rather than travel through Samaria.

Jesus, on the other hand, shows us that love knows no boundaries, recognises no inferior races and will have no truck with artificial excuses for a lack of humanity. (Peter later learned this at first hand when he saw a vision relating to unclean food, Acts 10:9–16.) When we look into our own hearts, the idea of the neighbour which Jesus is teaching here can present us with a challenge. Perhaps this is because Jesus is asking us to be good to our neighbours by treating them as we would like to be treated ourselves. He looks at the reality of what we are.

Meditation

(John 4:1–30)

THE WOMAN AT THE WELL

Today, when I went to the well as I always do,
something unusual happened.
I met a man who knew me
although I had never seen him before.
The moment he spoke, I could tell he was someone special.
It wasn't so much what he said
but how he spoke and what he understood.
He made me talk and tell the truth.
He said things that were amazing.
Suddenly I could see a whole new way of life.
He offered me a choice,
the possibility of a different future.
He was the first man I've met who gave me something

and looked for nothing in return.
I told the whole village and they listened,
when usually they ignore me.
They went to see for themselves
and agreed this man was different.
Suddenly we all have a choice
because we now know
we should not see Jews as our enemies –
and that changes everything.

Discussion

As a group, discuss whether you are conscious of problems aris-
ing from differences in background within your social circle,
workplace or society as a whole. How often do such differences
crop up and how do you cope with them?

Life

Spend a few minutes thinking about your own attitude towards
those of a different background from your own. Then undertake
the following analysis of your reflections. Does it make such a
difference?

Myself

Do I try to avoid contact with those of a different background
from my own?

Am I conscious of any fear or hostility within myself towards
those of a different background?

Others

Have I ever benefited from involvement with those of a different background?

Am I ever conscious of fear or hostility towards me from those of a different background from mine?

Response

Discuss with the group anything from your reflections that has particularly struck you. Share together any difficult experiences you may have had relating to those from other backgrounds. Pray together for God's healing to bring freedom from any feelings of prejudice or hurt.

Key question

Are there things I can do to better equip myself to deal with social, cultural, racial and religious differences when I meet them?

Praise

Leader: Lord, where can I go from your spirit?

All: Your hand will always guide me.

Leader: If I rise on the wings of the dawn...

All: Your hand will always guide me.

Leader: If I settle on the farthest shore...

All: Your right hand will hold me fast.

(Based on Psalm 139:7–10)

Meditation

Your skin is black
and in the dark you're blacker.
Your eyes are white
and in the dark are whiter.
Your laugh is loud
and in the dark it seems all round me.
Why don't I turn on the light
and see what you're really like?

Readings for the week

4. Choosing to respect those who are different		
Reflection	Day 5	Acts 17:1–9, The price of welcoming
	Day 6	Ephesians 2:1–22, Jews and Gentiles are brothers in Christ
	Day 7	Ephesians 3:14–21, Praying for others

5. Choosing to value relationships		
Preparation	Day 1	2 Corinthians 6:1–18, Fellowship, hardship and unbelief
	Day 2	1 John 1:1–10, Fellowship with one another and with God
	Day 3	Philippians 2:1–11, Fellowship with Jesus
Meeting	**Day 4**	**Matthew 12:46–50, Jesus' choice**

Session 5

Choosing to value relationships

Aim
To explore the place of family, close friendships and community in our lives.

Way in
Talk with your neighbour for a few minutes about your view of yourself in relation to those close to you. Then spend time praying together about the issues raised, or anything else you or your partner wish to bring before God.

Songs to sing
'Abba Father', MP 3, SOF 1, LP 1.
'Abide with me', MP 4, SOF 2.
'As the deer', MP 37, SOF 27.
'Bind us together', MP 54, SOF 43, LP 12.
'Blest be the tie that binds', MP 60.
'Brother, let me be your servant', SOF 54.
'Father God, I wonder', MP 128, SOF 92, LP 30.
'Father, I place into your hands', MP 133, SOF 97.
'Forth in the peace of Christ', LP 38.
'We worship God', LP 218.
'Wind, wind, blow on me', MP 771, SOF 609.

Music to listen to
Rachmaninov: 'Ave Maria', from *Agnus Dei*.

Mozart: Piano Concerto No. 21 K. 467, (Andante, 'Elvira Madigan'), from *Silence*.
Adiemus: 'Cantus Iterastus', from *Songs of Sanctuary*.

Bible

Matthew 12:46–50, Jesus' choice
46 While he was still speaking to the crowds, his mother and his brothers were standing outside, wanting to speak to him. 47 Someone told him, 'Look, your mother and your brothers are standing outside, wanting to speak to you.' 48 But to the one who had told him this, Jesus replied, 'Who is my mother, and who are my brothers?' 49 And pointing to his disciples, he said, 'Here are my mother and my brothers! 50 For whoever does the will of my Father in heaven is my brother and sister and mother.'

The choice of faith
Sometimes the pull of family ties or close relationships can tempt us to compromise our faith. For example, we may too easily believe we can bring round to our point of view someone with whom we want to form a relationship, just because that is what we desire; and so we begin to build on unsound foundations. This can turn out for the best but often does not, and we may be persuaded to dilute our principles or our faith in order to accommodate someone who does not feel as we do.

Jesus draws our attention first and foremost to the need to be in fellowship with those who are like-minded in faith. The test we are asked to apply is to determine whether or not we are alongside those whose prime purpose is to do the will of God. By implication, those who would draw us away from that purpose, be they family or friends, will have different objectives from ours; and our fellowship with them will not be based on our faith and its purpose.

St Paul tells us that we are to be 'conformed to the image of his [God's] Son' (Romans 8:29). This may point us in a different direction from those we are close to, if they do not choose to see Jesus as we do. That was the choice which confronted James and John (Matthew 4:18–22).

Meditation

(Matthew 4:18–22)

JAMES AND JOHN CHOOSE

The only life we have known surrounds the sea.
We know its moods and its meanness.
Over the years we have learned the places to fish
and the places to leave alone,
we have discovered respect and a sense of peace.
Our family has lived in the same house
beside the sea of Galilee for as long as anyone can remember.
When the old men tell their stories,
there's usually something that includes the family of Zebedee.
There has never been any question about what to do,
where to work or live.
It was always understood, as Zebedee's sons,
we would work on his boat
and live in the house of our forefathers –
we never thought any more about it.
Then one morning, when we're working on the nets,
along come our friends, Peter and Andrew
– brothers like us –
with a man called Jesus.
'Come with me,' he says as he walks by.
It's as if all our lives we've been waiting for this moment,
this hour, this one day,
when years of predictable tradition could change for ever.
We had to choose between the life
that had fallen on our shoulders
like a well-worn cloak, and this man.
We had heard of him but there had never been time,
what with the boat and the family,
to meet or listen to him.
Now we suddenly had a choice,
something new, a way out we had not seen before,
and Peter and Andrew had chosen it,
so why not us?

Discussion

How important is your family in your life? When you think of family, do you think primarily of blood ties?

Life

Jesus says, 'Abide in me as I abide in you' (John 15:4). This challenges us to question where Jesus figures when we think of family. The following questions may help you explore the relationship between family and fellowship in your life.

Important relationships

Myself

Who are the most important people in my life?

Who do I include when I think of family?

Others

How do I choose those with whom I am in fellowship?

How does that choice relate to my view of family?

How would I answer Jesus' question, 'Who is my mother, and who are my brothers?'

Response

Discuss together any significant features of life with your family or fellowship which have emerged from this exercise. Pray for relationships that have gone wrong, or which may be hindering the faith of individuals in the group. Give thanks for those in which family members are being drawn into fellowship with Jesus.

Key question

Who plays the leading role in my family and how does it show? Are there any choices I can make that will make the position of Jesus in my family life clearer than it is?

Praise

Leader: God is light.

All: In him there is no darkness at all.

Leader: Seek fellowship with him.

All: In him there is no darkness at all.

Leader: Seek fellowship with one another.

All: Let us walk in the light.

Leader: You will fill me with joy in your presence.

(Based on I John 1:5–7)

Meditation

Today has been a good day.
I have collected a great deal of money, paid off the Romans,
taken my bonus and had a good lunch.
Jerusalem is in a state of excitement.
A man called Jesus is coming to the city.
There are a lot of men named Jesus,
just as there are a lot of men called Matthew,
but this one is special.
Some say he is a great healer,
others that he is the best teacher they have ever heard.
Some even say he is the Messiah.
I don't know about any of this because I've never seen him,
but it is intriguing.

They say Jesus has recruited quite a few fishermen as followers.
Isn't it odd that under-educated fishermen are chosen,
not people who can read and write,
who are good with figures – like me?
But I'm regarded as a traitor – I work with the Romans.
People call me a publican
and won't have anything to do with me.
So I mix with my own kind and shrug my shoulders.

Suddenly the street is full of people.
There he is standing in front of my table, looking at me.
It feels as though he can see right into my heart.
He says, 'Matthew, you don't need all this.
Leave it and follow me.'
Just like that, I have been chosen.

I'm not family, I'm not a friend, I'm not even from Nazareth,
yet he has chosen me.
I don't know why I'm doing it, but I leave my table and I follow.
I have made my choice,
for he has chosen me to be his brother.

Readings for the week

5. Choosing to value relationships		
Reflection	Day 5	Luke 9:51–62, Following Jesus or family
	Day 6	John 8:31–41, The children of Abraham
	Day 7	Galatians 6:1–10, The family of believers

6. Personal choices - Jesus' and ours		
Preparation	Day 1	John 5:31–44, Choosing Jesus
	Day 2	John 7:14–18, Choosing God's will
	Day 3	1 Peter 1:13–25, Choosing the truth
Meeting	**Day 4**	**John 11:1–44, Jesus and Lazarus**

Session 6

Personal choices –
Jesus' and ours

Aim
To look at the way we handle conflicting priorities.

Way in
With a neighbour, look at one area in your life where you have a choice to make at the present moment, and how you are approaching it. Then spend time praying together about this or anything else you or your partner wish to bring before God.

Songs to sing
'Alleluia! Alleluia!', SOF 5.
'All hail, King Jesus', MP 11, SOF 7.
'I have decided to follow Jesus', MP 272, LP 76.
'I heard the voice of Jesus say', MP 275, SOF 215.
'Praise You, Lord', MP 565, SOF 472.
'The Servant King', MP 162, SOF 120, LP 40.
'You laid aside Your majesty', MP 795, SOF 633, LP 230.
'When I survey the wondrous cross', MP 755, SOF 596, LP 221.

Music to listen to
Barber: 'Agnus Dei' (Adagio for Strings), from *Agnus Dei*.
Tavener: 'Alleluia' (Song for Athene), from *Silence*.
Enya: 'Angeles', from *Shepherd Moons*.

Bible

John 11:1–44, Jesus and Lazarus

11 Now a certain man was ill, Lazarus of Bethany, the village of Mary and her sister Martha. 2 Mary was the one who anointed the Lord with perfume and wiped his feet with her hair; her brother Lazarus was ill. 3 So the sisters sent a message to Jesus, 'Lord, he whom you love is ill.' 4 But when Jesus heard it, he said, 'This illness does not lead to death; rather it is for God's glory, so that the Son of God may be glorified through it.' 5 Accordingly, though Jesus loved Martha and her sister and Lazarus, 6 after having heard that Lazarus was ill, he stayed two days longer in the place where he was.

7 Then after this he said to the disciples, 'Let us go to Judea again.' 8 The disciples said to him, 'Rabbi, the Jews were just now trying to stone you, and you are going there again?' 9 Jesus answered, 'Are there not twelve hours of daylight? Those who walk during the day do not stumble, because they see the light of this world. 10 But those who walk at night stumble, because the light is not in them.' 11 After saying this, he told them, 'Our friend Lazarus has fallen asleep, but I am going there to awaken him.' 12 The disciples said to him, 'Lord, if he has fallen asleep, he will be all right.' 13 Jesus, however, had been speaking about his death, but they thought that he was referring merely to sleep. 14 Then Jesus told them plainly, 'Lazarus is dead. 15 For your sake I am glad I was not there, so that you may believe. But let us go to him.' 16 Thomas, who was called the Twin, said to his fellow disciples, 'Let us also go, that we may die with him.'

17 When Jesus arrived, he found that Lazarus had already been in the tomb four days. 18 Now Bethany was near Jerusalem, some two miles away, 19 and many of the Jews had come to Martha and Mary to console them about their brother. 20 When Martha heard that Jesus was coming, she went and met him, while Mary stayed at home. 21 Martha said to Jesus, 'Lord, if you had been here, my brother would not have died. 22 But even now I know that God will give you whatever you ask of him.' 23 Jesus said to her, 'Your brother will rise again.' 24 Martha said to him, 'I know that he will

rise again in the resurrection on the last day.' 25 Jesus said to her, 'I am the resurrection and the life. Those who believe in me, even though they die, will live, 26 and everyone who lives and believes in me will never die. Do you believe this?' 27 She said to him, 'Yes, Lord, I believe that you are the Messiah, the Son of God, the one coming into the world.'

28 When she had said this, she went back and called her sister Mary, and told her privately, 'The Teacher is here and is calling for you.' 29 And when she heard it, she got up quickly and went to him. 30 Now Jesus had not yet come to the village, but was still at the place where Martha had met him. 31 The Jews who were with her in the house, consoling her, saw Mary get up quickly and go out. They followed her because they thought that she was going to the tomb to weep there. 32 When Mary came where Jesus was and saw him, she knelt at his feet and said to him, 'Lord, if you had been here, my brother would not have died.' 33 When Jesus saw her weeping, and the Jews who came with her also weeping, he was greatly disturbed in spirit and deeply moved. 34 He said, 'Where have you laid him?' They said to him, 'Lord, come and see.' 35 Jesus began to weep. 36 So the Jews said, 'See how he loved him!' 37 But some of them said, 'Could not he who opened the eyes of the blind man have kept this man from dying?'

38 Then Jesus, again greatly disturbed, came to the tomb. It was a cave, and a stone was lying against it. 39 Jesus said, 'Take away the stone.' Martha, the sister of the dead man, said to him, 'Lord, already there is a stench because he has been dead four days.' 40 Jesus said to her, 'Did I not tell you that if you believed, you would see the glory of God?' 41 So they took away the stone. And Jesus looked upward and said, 'Father, I thank you for having heard me. 42 I knew that you always hear me, but I have said this for the sake of the crowd standing here, so that you may believe that you sent me.' 43 When he had said this, he cried with a loud voice, 'Lazarus, come out!' 44 The dead man came out, his hands and feet bound with strips of cloth, and his face wrapped in a cloth. Jesus said to them, 'Unbind him, and let him go.'

45 Many of the Jews therefore, who had come with Mary and had seen what Jesus did, believed in him. 46 But some of them

went to the Pharisees and told them what he had done. [47] So the chief priest and the Pharisees called a meeting of the council, and said, 'What are we to do? This man is performing many signs.'

The choice of glory

At first sight it seems rather shocking that Jesus should delay in his response to the plea for help by Mary and Martha on behalf of their brother Lazarus. After all, not only was Lazarus dear to Jesus as a friend but he would also know how important Lazarus was to his sisters as the male in the household. However, Jesus waited two more days before setting out for Bethany.

Obviously, the disciples were concerned for Jesus' safety, since Bethany was so close to Jerusalem and the Pharisees were not kindly disposed towards him. When they arrived at Bethany, they met not only Martha and Mary but also a sizeable crowd who had come from Jerusalem to console them. It was therefore a significant audience which witnessed the raising of Lazarus from the dead.

For those who believed in Jesus, the death of Lazarus would have looked like a disaster that could have been avoided. Then it was transformed into a glorious triumph. A week or so later, Calvary appeared to be the end of all hope; a few days after that, it became the glory of the resurrection. We must, in making our choices, look beneath surface appearances to the eternal reality.

Meditation

AT THE CROSSROADS

What lies before me is a choice –
to walk away, leave Jerusalem
and disappear into the countryside I know so well,
or to carry on to Jerusalem and face death.
Gradually, as the last three years have passed
since Cana and that wedding where it all began,
I have become more aware of a purpose.
Perhaps I have always known
that once the Pharisees saw me as a threat

they would have to kill me – but crucifixion!
I had not faced the reality of it until now –
confronted by what it would actually mean
to leave my friends and family
and to deal with dying on my own.
If I am honest, I didn't know
how much being here had come to mean to me –
the routine and the challenge,
the journeys and the places in which I have stayed
and been made welcome.
It all came home to me in Bethany last week.
My Father showed me, through my friend Lazarus,
how it would be for me –
except that I will die in public but alone.
Now, tonight, I can feel loneliness gathering round me.
We were happy together in that upper room over supper.
Now it is dark and cold and they can't stay awake.
The evil one is closing their eyes,
so they can't keep watch with me or over themselves.
I must not think beyond here and now.
It is always in this present moment that decisions are made,
and I have made mine.
I choose to accept the path my Father has chosen.
To Him be the glory.

Discussion
How do you manage to cope with conflicting choices?

Life

Most of us are confronted from time to time with choices to which
there is no absolutely right or wrong answer. Sometimes the decision which we know is best is nevertheless very painful. Use the
following questions to help you think, under the guidance of the
Holy Spirit, about the way in which you address difficult choices.
If you are facing such a problem at present, use it as an example.

How do I choose?

Myself

Do I take account of both my thoughts and my feelings about the issues involved?

Do I present my thoughts and feelings to God?

Others

Do I test the choice I believe is right against the thoughts and feelings of others?

Do I consider how right my choice feels at this moment when I reflect on those involved?

Response

Are there any particular aspects of decision-making which can be shared with the group in order to gain a wider perspective? As a group, pray through any difficult areas that come to light.

Key question

Do I spend enough time with God looking at the outcome of difficult choices, either in gratitude or to digest difficult lessons?

Praise

Leader: Jesus says, 'Remain in my love.'
All: Help us to be obedient.
Leader: Jesus says, 'Obey my commands.'
All: Help us to be obedient.
Leader: Jesus lays down his life for his friends.
All: Help us to love one another.

(Based on John 15:9,13)

Meditation

Receive the gift of faith from One who chooses to give it.
Nurture it with the living water of hope,
guard it against your doubts and fears,
feed it with the knowledge
that it opens the way to an eternity
untouched by time.

Thus will it grow into the love
of the One who gave it, and bear fruit.
This love, through grace, you can choose to give away
just as you chose to receive it.

Readings for the week

6. Personal choices – Jesus and ours		
Reflection	Day 5	John 15:9–17, Jesus chooses us
	Day 6	John 13:12–20, Jesus knows the chosen
	Day 7	Matthew 7:15–23, Jesus knows the sincere believer

Further resources from Scripture Union

'I am...' Six studies in John's Gospel for groups
Tony Kidd
A six-week course which gives a deeper understanding of the claims Jesus made about himself in John's Gospel, exploring their significance for us as Christians, individually and as part of his Body, the church. An ideal course for Lent. 1 85999 176 9, £3.99

At the Foot of the Cross
Tony Kidd
These six studies, following Jesus from Gethsemane to the Emmaus road, aim to engage participants in the events and help them respond creatively and practically. Suitable for individuals as well as groups, and is ideal for Lent. 1 85999 247 1, £3.99

Through the Bible in a Year: A spiritual journal
Dennis Lennon
A completely original syllabus, constructed around eleven themes, gives an overarching picture of the whole Bible story. Includes space for keeping a record of your spiritual journey. 1 85999 196 3, £9.99

How to Read the Bible for all its Worth (2nd ed)
Gordon D Fee and Douglas Stuart
This in-depth guide to interpreting the Bible is consistently popular and fast becoming a classic. 0 86201 974 5, £7.50

Be an Expert (in 137 minutes) in Interpreting the Bible
Richard Briggs
A short, entertaining and informative guide to biblical interpretation (hermeneutics). With humour and clarity, Richard Briggs outlines biblical genre and other difficult concepts in a way that ordinary people can understand. 1 85999 224 2, £3.99

How Can I Hear God?
Gillian Peall
Does God really speak to us? Do we have to be special people to hear him? How can we be sure that it is God who is speaking to us? Gillian Peall draws from her own experiences and from the examples of people who have heard God speak - from the Bible, from the past and from contemporary life - to explore the ways in which God communicates with us and how we can become better at hearing him. 1 85999 293 5, £3.99

Life's Like That
Jeanette Henderson
Brimming with warmth and humour, these anecdotes offer a fresh perspective on selected Bible passages. The author draws on her experiences of family life in this country, and short-term missions in Africa, to show how we can learn to see God at work in the ups and down of everyday life. 1 85999 311 7, £4.99

Closer to God: Practical help on your spiritual journey
Ian Bunting (ed)
We're all on a journey through life, with God. For many it is a struggle. What may help us? In this book, members of the Grove Spirituality Group write from personal experience, and from their understanding of the way Christians have come closer to God down the centuries. 0 86201 550 2, £5.99

How to Pray When Life Hurts
Roy Lawrence
Prayer makes a difference because God makes a difference. Whether we feel guilty or angry, fearful or under pressure, this

book offers practical help on how to pray when life hurts. 0 86201 969 9, £5.99

Make Me a Channel
Roy Lawrence
This book highlights the struggle many Christians have in achieving the balance between receiving from God and giving to others. But we need to do both to be any good at either. Without God's input, our good intentions flounder; but if we don't share his gifts, we are not being the people he wants us to be. 1 85999 015 0, £4.99

Walking Backwards: Dealing with guilt
Jeff Lucas
Are you struggling with things you've repented of but can't forget? It is God's will for you to turn, face the future and leave the past finally and completely behind. Written in a lively, anecdotal style, this is a down-to-earth book on forgiveness. 0 86201 973 7, £4.99

Weak Enough for God to Use
Dennis Lennon
Biblical inspiration for Christians, to encourage them to believe that God uses ordinary people to do mighty things for him. Includes character studies of Mary, Moses, David and Jeremiah among others, as well as contemporary accounts of people who have made an impact on the world around them. 1 85999 290 0, £4.99

Finding a Spiritual Friend
Timothy Jones
Every Christian needs the support and encouragement that comes with meaningful spiritual friendship. This inspirational guide shows the reader how to go about establishing these relationships, drawing on the author's personal experience and a combination of biblical examples, classical writings, contemporary stories and guidance on prayer. 1 85999 336 2, £4.99

Spiritual Encounter Guides

Stephen D and Jacalyn Eyre

A fresh approach to personal devotion for new or long-time Christians, the aim of these Bible studies is to help readers find intimacy with God. Each book contains one month's Bible reading material. £3.50 each.

Abiding in Christ's Love, 1 85999 021 5
Sinking Your Roots in Christ, 1 85999 022 3
Sitting at the Feet of Jesus, 1 85999 020 7
Waiting on the Lord, 1 85999 019 3

Tune In

A superb concept in audio cassettes. Clips from the Bible and contemporary Christian music blend with the voices of well-known Christians and ordinary people to bring a fresh perspective to key Bible texts. Easy listening for car journeys, or a thought-provoking opener for quiet times or group Bible studies. Both double cassette packages, £8.99 each.

Tune in to the Beatitudes, 1 85999 092 4
Tune in to the Fruit of the Spirit, 1 85999 093 2

All these titles are available from your local Christian bookshop, or from SU Mail Order, PO Box 764, Oxford, OX4 5FJ; tel (01865) 716880, fax (01865) 715152.